DUS...ON LIBRARY SERVICE

tate

/126

me.htm

KT-405-484

Building History
MEDIEVAL CASTLE

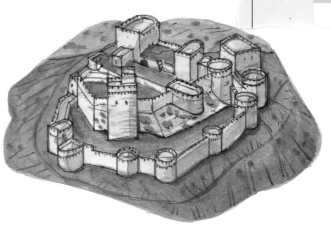

Gillian Clements

W
FRANKLIN WATTS
LONDON • SYDNEY

First published in 2006 by
Franklin Watts
338 Euston Road
London
NW1 3BH

Franklin Watts Australia
Hachette Children's Books
Level 17/207 Kent Street
Sydney NSW 2000

© Gillian Clements 2006

CHESHIRE
LIBRARIES

17 NOV 2006

RL

Editor: Adrian Cole
Art Director: Jonathan Hair
Consultant: Chris Gravett, former Senior Curator,
Royal Armouries, Tower of London

ISBN-10: 0-7496-6354-5
ISBN-13: 978-0-7496-6354-4

Dewey Classification: 728.8'10902

A CIP catalogue record for this book is available
from the British Library.

All rights reserved. No part of this publication may be
reproduced, stored in a retrieval system, or transmitted
in any form or by any means, electronic, mechanical,
photocopy, recording or otherwise, without the prior
written permission of the copyright owner.

Printed in Malaysia

Franklin Watts is a division of Hachette Children's Books

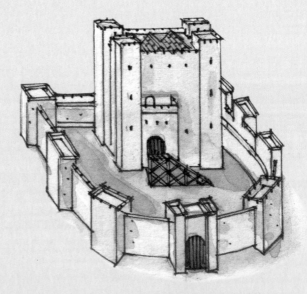

Contents

6-7   What is a medieval castle?

8-9   Who ruled in medieval times?

10-11   Who built the castles?

12-13   How did they build a keep?

14-15   Who lived in the castle?

16-17   Where were the castles built?

18-19   How were castles improved?

20-21   What was a concentric castle?

22-23   What happened under a siege?

24-25   How did soldiers defend castles?

26-27   Where are the old castles?

28   Timeline

29   Glossary

30   Index

What is a medieval castle?

In medieval times, castles were the fortified homes of kings and important lords. They were built to be very strong so that their owner and his household were safe from enemy attack.

When were the great ages of castle building?

The medieval period, or the Middle Ages (c.1000–1500 CE), was one of the busiest periods in history for building castles. However, castles and forts have been built throughout the ages. Medieval castle designs were influenced by earlier castles.

ENGLAND

FRANCE

SPAIN

ITALY

NORTH AFRICA

THE HOLY LAND (Palestine)

In the 8th century, Muslim Moors from North Africa invaded Spain. They built strong stone castles to resist rebellions in the areas they controlled.

In the 11th century, Normans from France conquered England, and built wooden and stone castles to help break English and Welsh resistance. Normans invaded southern Italy too, building strong stone towers there.

One of the greatest ages of castle building followed Europe's Christian Crusades to the Holy Land (11th–13th century). The great Crusader castles inspired new concentric castle designs across Europe.

Why did people build castles?

The kings and lords who built castles used them as bases from which to control their land and people. During times of war, castles protected them and their family from attackers. Kings and lords also built castles to show how big and powerful they were.

◀ Edward I used castles to help with his invasion of Wales.

▶ William the Conqueror built castles in England after his invasion from France.

What were castles like?

▶ 8th century Moorish castles – Almodóvar del Rio is a hilltop fortress in Córdoba, Spain. It has square towers and is surrounded by a moat.

▶ 11th century Norman timber motte and bailey castles – none of these structures survive, although many of the earth mounds do.

◀ 12th century keeps – Castle Burbant, Henegouwen, the Netherlands. This 20-metre high square keep has four-metre thick walls. A stone curtain wall was added in the 14th century.

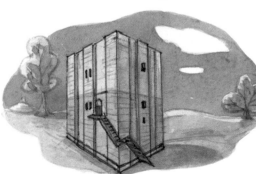

◀ 13th century concentric castles – Krak des Chevaliers, Syria. A castle existed on this site from the 11th century, but it was rebuilt c.1205 and became one of the world's greatest castles.

▶ 13th–14th century luxury castles – Coucy-le-Chateau (ruin), France. The stone castle on this site was built by Enguerrand III, Lord of Coucy. Its central tower stood 60 metres tall!

Who ruled in medieval times?

Kings and lords ruled over all other people in a medieval society. People were bound together by ties of duty and loyalty, which created a strict social order called a feudal society.

What is a feudal society?

Feudal society developed in Western Europe from the 5th century CE, after the collapse of the Roman Empire. People came under the rule and protection of a local lord or king. In return, the people had to fight in wars for him, pay him taxes, or work his land.

I'm the king of the castle...

The King was the head of feudal society. He could grant land to a lord to build a castle on, but he expected loyalty in return. The king had many castles.

The lord (or baron) lived in a castle with his family. He sent soldiers and supplies when the king needed them. Lords also took care of the needs of those below them – especially their knights.

I serve my king.

I serve my lord and the king.

Knights and soldiers were skilled fighters. They served their lord in many ways, but mainly by going into battle for him.

Peasants (villeins, cottars and serfs) could not leave their lord's land. However, they could farm the land if they paid their lord a 'feudal tax', usually some of their produce. Cottars had small cottages with approximately 12 hectares of land. Very rarely, peasants could save enough money to buy their freedom. More often they escaped to find work in a town.

Who's who in the church?

In medieval times the Church was very powerful and a very rich landowner, rivalling the importance of a king and his lords. The church hierarchy, as in the feudal system, had many levels.

The Archbishop was in charge of the land's most important cathedral. He appointed the bishops, and sometimes his power could rival the king's.

The Bishop, a senior clergyman, was in charge of many parishes – and his own cathedral. He might visit important lords and kings in nearby castles.

Abbots/Abbesses and Priors/Prioresses were the heads of abbeys or priories of monks and nuns. They were almost as important as bishops.

Priests were the ordinary people's local religious leaders, appointed to their church and parish by a bishop. A castle might also be in a priest's parish.

Chaplains were priests of lords' private chapels. These chapels were often created within the safety of the lord's castle.

Who's who in the town?

Medieval towns became centres for merchants, traders and craftsmen. People could use their skills to work their way to a better life. Some towns were protected by a nearby castle, or fortified with a surrounding wall.

The mayor was the powerful head of the town or city's ruling council.

Merchants traded in the town, and might also visit the local castle to sell their wares.

Master craftsmen were members of a particular craft who had gained the top position in their trade.

Apprentices learnt a craft, under instruction from a master craftsman to whom they were 'bound' for as many as seven years of instruction.

Who built the castles?

Only the richest and most powerful men, like kings and wealthy lords, had the money to build a great castle. Building castles required many fine craftsmen.

Who ordered the building?

Very wealthy people, such as kings, ordered castles to be built. Good stone for high, thick walls and wood for scaffolding were very expensive materials. Wages cost a lot too. At the beginning of the reconquest of Spain from the Moors in c.1440, King Juan II of Castile ordered his treasurer to build the magnificent Fuensaldaña castle in north-central Spain.

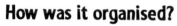
▲ King Alfonso VI of Castile built the Alcazár of Segovia in Spain in the 11th century.

How was it organised?

A huge amount of organisation was needed to build a castle. Officers of the king or lord had to buy building materials, find labourers, pay them and supervise their work.

These labourers are completing the base of a keep.

Was castle building seasonal?

The simplest timber castle in Western Europe usually took 6–9 months to finish, depending on the weather. Stone castles took a lot longer to complete, some as long as 8–10 years! They needed warm sunshine to harden the mortar between the huge blocks of stone, and dry dirt roads to move heavy equipment and building materials.

Craftsmen and labourers weren't always paid on time. In protest, they sometimes stopped work. At the Builth Wells castle site in Wales in 1282, angry workers downed tools because of the 'want of money'.

Who did the work?

Hundreds of people helped to build a castle. In addition to the unskilled labouring men, a wide variety of skilled craftsmen were paid to work on these great projects. They were hired from all parts of the country, and even travelled from abroad.

Master mason

The master mason was a skilled and experienced stonemason, and also the castle's architect. Many master masons travelled throughout Britain and Europe where their skills were highly prized.

Stonemasons

Stonemasons were skilled in choosing stone from a quarry and cutting it to shape. They earned money working on important castles, which took years to finish. Strong stone walls were vital to castle building.

Wooden hoists were used to lift up heavy blocks of stone.

Carpenters

Carpenters helped make scaffolding (vital for building). They also cut timber for the floors and rafters in the finished castle.

Ditchers

The best ditchers came from flat, wet areas, like East Anglia in England, and from the Low Countries (now The Netherlands). They dug the castle's foundations, its moat and any other important ditches and ramparts.

Around 2,000–3,000 men worked at Edward I's three Welsh sites – at Caernarfon, Conway and Harlech – 1,000 men at Harlech (1286 CE) alone. Beaumaris, Edward's great, unfinished castle on Anglesey (1295 CE), needed 3,500 men.

How did they build a keep?

Between the 11th and 13th centuries, many kings and lords chose to live in tall, incredibly strong, stone keeps. Their stone walls and first floor entrances were secure against fire and direct attack.

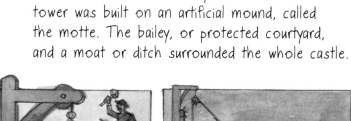

Motte

Bailey

Where were keeps built?

Castle design varied from place to place as skills improved. Some stone keeps replaced motte and bailey castles. They were built on solid ground. Other keeps were built high up on rocky hills.

▲ Motte and bailey castles were first built by the Normans in the 11th century. The main timber tower was built on an artificial mound, called the motte. The bailey, or protected courtyard, and a moat or ditch surrounded the whole castle.

What was the building process?

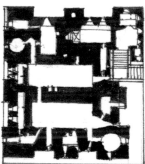

Castle site plans are draw up.

Masons choose stone from a local quarry.

Masons cut and shape stone.

Carpenters put up scaffolding as the walls get higher.

Main walls are solid stone on the outside with loose stone in the middle.

The windows are cut and shaped from stone.

The castle's water source is protected, and usually made into a well.

A timber framed roof is covered with slates, lead or wooden tiles.

What was the keep like?

The layout of the rooms in the keep varied. Some had formal uses, while others had more space for private apartments.

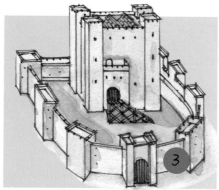

Glass was rare, even in the 14th century, but see-through oiled linen screens kept out the worst window draughts.

1. Windows

Slit windows on the lower floors let in little light, but made it difficult for attackers to shoot arrows inside.

2. Walls

A keep had very thick walls. Small bedchambers, closets and latrines, and the spiral stairs linking floors, were built within them. The walls were high, too – later ones had many floors.

3. Curtain wall

Master masons designed sentry walks, gatehouses and arrow loops to make the curtain walls secure against attack.

I'm a prisoner. Get me out of here!

4. Entrance and stairs

The staircase up to the first floor was made of wood or stone. The entrance was too high for raiders to attack with a battering ram.

5. Great hall

This was a large and important public room. It was heated by a huge fireplace and may have been located on the first or second floor.

6. Kitchens

Some keeps had kitchens next to the hall, so food preparation was close to where it was eaten. Kitchens were sometimes put in a separate building, because of the risk of fire.

7. Stores

Cool, dark rooms in the keep's basement where stores of food and wine were kept.

8. Well

A source of fresh water from underground, usually inside the castle keep.

Who lived in the castle?

The castle was the lord's private home, a base for his soldiers and knights and a centre for local government. A feudal king travelled from one of his castles to another, so someone had to run the castle when he was away.

The castle household: What did they do?

The household could be large – up to 50 people. But when the lord was away, only a small number stayed behind to run the castle.

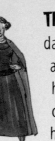

The lord watched over all the formal parts of daily life, such as managing his castle and lands, and sitting in court. When he had time, he went hunting. His lady tended the garden and created intricate embroidery, and also helped him and his steward run the castle.

The steward acted as the lord's deputy. He organised the household and controlled spending so the castle ran smoothly.

Knights were well-trained mounted soldiers from wealthy families. They practised their fighting skills daily and went hunting with their lord.

Squires (apprentice knights) were young boys from rich families. They served the knights, and some became knights themselves when they were older.

Men-at-arms were well-trained soldiers. They lived at the castle, but were not the equals of the knights.

Servants

including cooks, maids, grooms, falconers and huntsmen were as important to the smooth running of the castle as the steward himself.

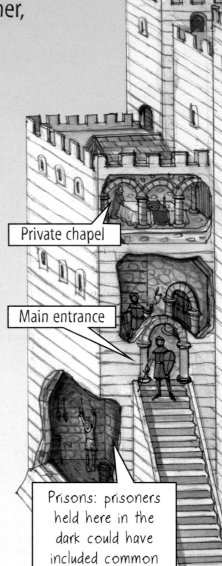

Private chapel

Main entrance

Prisons: prisoners held here in the dark could have included common thieves and nobles.

What was the lord's daily life?

Waking – dressing – shaving

In the garderobe (a private latrine)

In the chapel for daily Mass

What was it like inside the castle?

Inside, the medieval castle was very bare – even though wealthy lords could afford more furniture and decoration. Also, because small windows let in very little light, it was dark and airless, especially in winter – and smelly too! There were few chances for people to wash.

Baths taken in tubs by the fire were unpopular in a cold castle. In 1209, King John took just 12 baths in the whole year!

Bedroom

Bedroom

People in the castle had to use latrines: pits with no flushing water. A projecting tower latrine ran straight into the moat or ditch.

Great hall

Kitchen

It's my job to keep the castle secure.

The constable lived in the castle with his family, and was responsible for its security.

Guard room

Guard room

The chaplain was the priest in charge of the castle's chapels.

Spiral stairs

The mason did building and repair work, when required.

Stores

Brewhouse for storing wine

Talking to the steward about food and drink supplies

Administration, inspecting land, seeing tenants

Eating lunch

Watching weapons training

Falconry and hunting rabbits, hares and deer

Feasting in the hall with guests

Prayers and bed

Where were the castles built?

The best place for a king or a lord to build his castle was on high ground, because that was the easiest place to defend. It also gave a good view of the area and approaching enemies.

Why were many castles built near water?

Many castles needed a fresh water supply from a river. It was also easier to transport the building materials by water than on dirt tracks. Castles were built to guard important waterways too, especially near the sea.

What was 'strategic planning'?

Some powerful medieval rulers planned and built a whole series of castles in territories they wanted to control and conquer. They chose positions high on hills that were easy to defend, or near important travelling routes that could be protected. The Moors successfully built strongholds in 8th century Spain (see below). Then, at the end of the 13th century in Wales, Edward I (reigned 1272–1307), helped England control Wales with a few strategically-placed castles.

In Britain, King Edward I's strategic castle building – planned and directed towards conquering Wales – was one of the biggest projects of its kind in all of Europe.

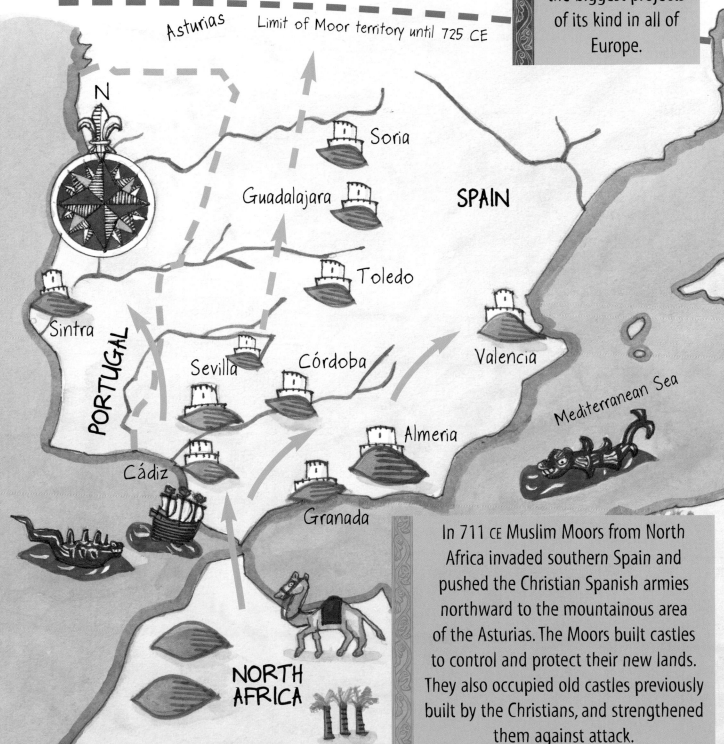

Asturias

Limit of Moor territory until 725 CE

N

Soria

Guadalajara

SPAIN

Toledo

Sintra

PORTUGAL

Sevilla

Córdoba

Valencia

Mediterranean Sea

Almeria

Cádiz

Granada

NORTH AFRICA

In 711 CE Muslim Moors from North Africa invaded southern Spain and pushed the Christian Spanish armies northward to the mountainous area of the Asturias. The Moors built castles to control and protect their new lands. They also occupied old castles previously built by the Christians, and strengthened them against attack.

How were castles improved?

Castle design continued to change and develop. They had
to be larger to hold more fighting men, and they had
to be stronger too, because attackers were
improving their weapons, and thinking up
new tactics. Old castles were
strengthened and
new castles were
built on old
sites.

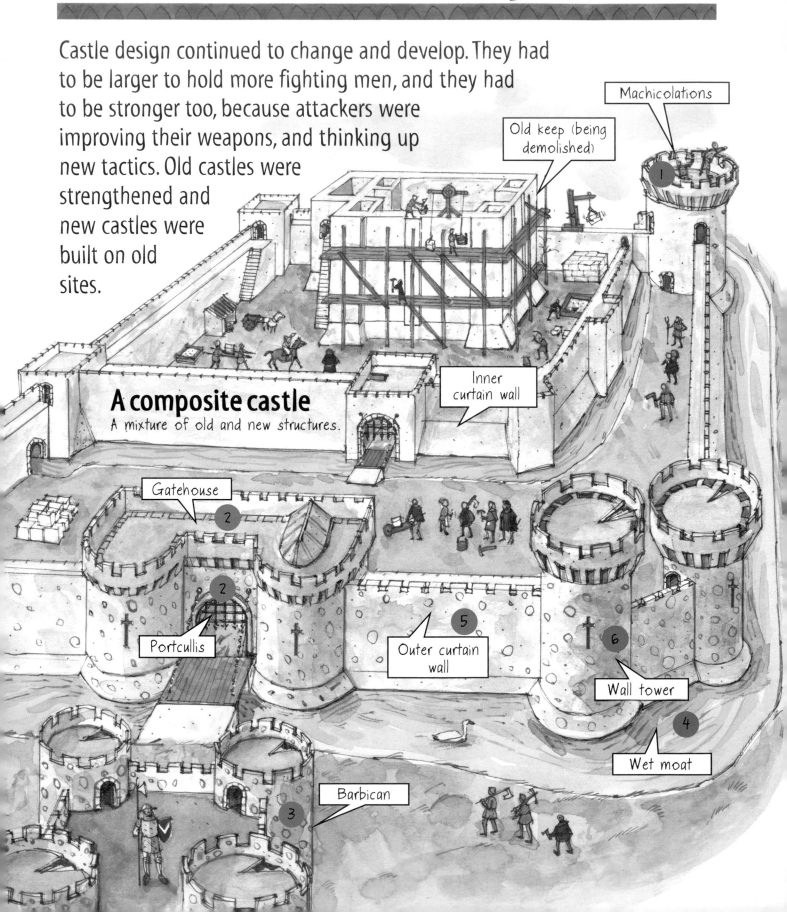

Machicolations

Old keep (being demolished)

Inner curtain wall

A composite castle
A mixture of old and new structures.

Gatehouse

Portcullis

Outer curtain wall

Wall tower

Wet moat

Barbican

What were the new ideas and additions?

1. Stone machicolations (right)

These features at the top of the wall helped defenders shoot or drop missiles onto the enemy below, without danger to themselves. Rounded corners also started to be used because they were stronger against direct attacks and undermining (see page 23).

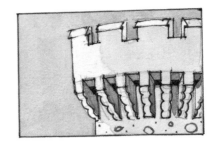

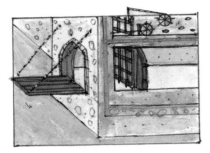

2. Gatehouse and portcullis (left)

The castle's main gatehouse – usually the point of attack – was strengthened with new defensive features. A portcullis was a strong iron grating that could be lowered to protect the castle's main door.

3. Barbican (right)

An outer defence beyond the gatehouse had all the features of the main gatehouse, and acted like a mini-keep.

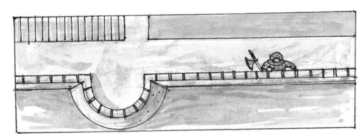

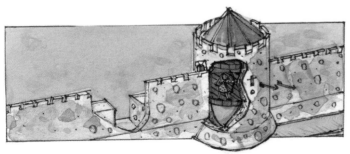

4. Wet moat

The flooded ditch deterred many enemies from attacking by direct assault, or by undermining.

5. Curtain walls

Inner and outer curtain walls surrounded the keep, often with enough space for buildings to be constructed between them.

6. Wall towers

Defenders could move between the wall towers along the protected castle wall-walk.

Where did they get the new technology?

The first Christian Crusade to the Holy Land to fight the Saracens (followers of Islam) began at the end of the 11th century. Crusaders returning to Europe from the Holy Land saw Crusader castles in lands like Syria and brought the advanced castle technology home.

◀ Crusader castles, such as Krak des Chevaliers, were the main inspiration for many castle improvements.

What was a concentric castle?

A concentric castle was cleverly designed to have many layers of defence. Attacking armies found this design nearly impossible to overcome. Every part of the castle was protected by another part, beginning with the outer curtain wall, its towers and the defended barbican – and ending with the strong inner defences.

Was it a new design?

Concentric castles had some of the features of older castles, but many were newly built. New concentric castles (as shown) had no keep. Master masons, with their mixture of ideas, had created a modern 13th century castle. They left no weak spot; a permanent garrison as small as 30 men could easily defend it.

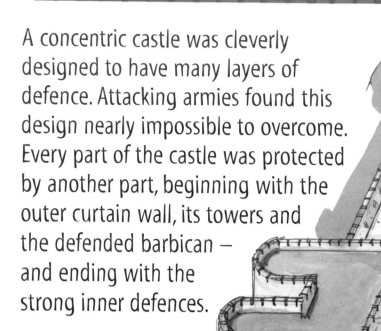

Massive curtain walls The concentric castle had thick curtain walls, a higher inner one and a lower outer one. A narrow strip of land between, called the outer bailey, could be easily defended.

Moat Around the outer curtain wall, this trench deterred access to the castle walls, and stopped enemies from undermining the walls.

Rounded wall corners

Masons introduced these because they were strong and could be easily defended.

Two heavily-defended gatehouses

The castle's main gatehouses – for the outer and inner curtain walls – had large twin flanking towers, from where defenders could shoot at attacking forces. The lord's family chambers were often housed on the top floor of one of the inner gatehouse's huge towers.

Wall towers

Defenders could shoot from the huge inner wall towers onto attackers beyond the lower outer curtain wall. The wall towers – built like mini-keeps – were used as accommodation, prison space and storage.

Continuous passageways through the curtain walls, like those at Beaumaris, gave defending soldiers safe access to any part of the castle, away from attackers' shots.

Master James of St George built many different castles in Wales – Rhuddlan, Flint, Conway, Caernarfon, Harlech and Beaumaris. Some designs were very like the castles he had seen on the Crusades. Edward I paid him 2–3 shillings a day, when the usual wage for a mason was 2 shillings a week! When James retired, the King promised him a generous pension.

What happened under a siege?

Concentric castles were well built. Often the only way for an attacker to break in and overpower the defenders was to lay siege to the castle. This involved surrounding the castle and blocking supplies. Siege machines were also used against the castle.

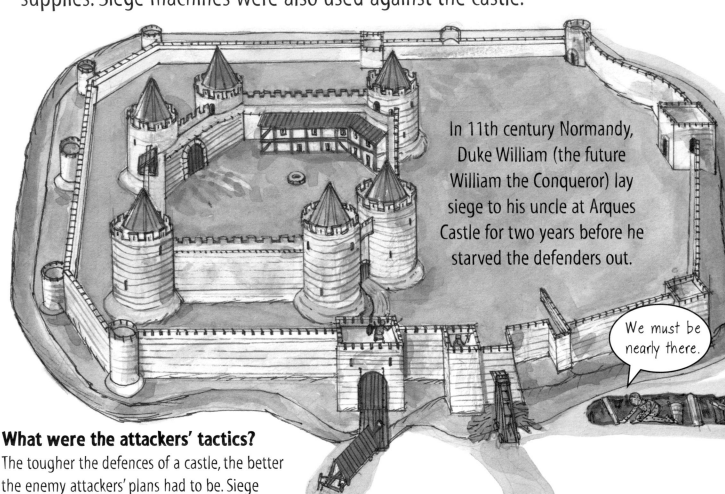

In 11th century Normandy, Duke William (the future William the Conqueror) lay siege to his uncle at Arques Castle for two years before he starved the defenders out.

We must be nearly there.

What were the attackers' tactics?

The tougher the defences of a castle, the better the enemy attackers' plans had to be. Siege tactics involved many different types of attack.

Bribery sometimes persuaded a defender to open a postern (back gate) and let the enemy in. Owain Glyndwr took the great Harlech Castle this way in 1404.

Battering rams (left) and fire attacks against the well-defended gates were dangerous. So soldiers used battering rams under a protective cover (a cat) to attack walls.

Timber towers (belfreys, left) were put up against the castle walls in a direct attack, and archers fired onto the curtain wall from them.

Bombardment

Bombarding the walls could breach them and let soldiers through. Siege machines, such as ballistas, were re-introduced from Roman times. Trebuchets and mangonels were also very effective.

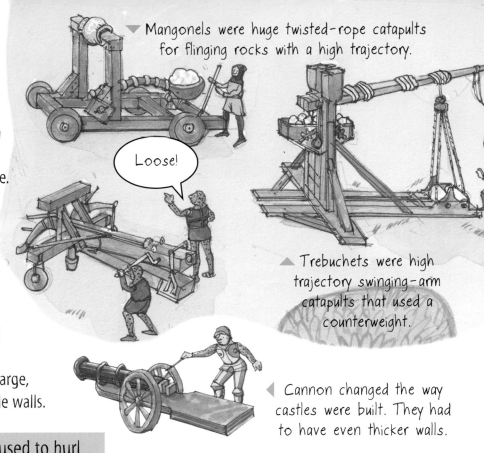

▼ Mangonels were huge twisted-rope catapults for flinging rocks with a high trajectory.

Loose!

▶ Ballistas were giant crossbows.

▲ Trebuchets were high trajectory swinging-arm catapults that used a counterweight.

Guns using gunpowder were experimented with in the 14th century. The French attacked Southampton in 1338, firing iron darts. 15th century cannon fired large, stone balls and could breach castle walls.

◀ Cannon changed the way castles were built. They had to have even thicker walls.

Siege machines were used to hurl lots of different missiles, from big stones, inflammable liquid and giant arrows, to horrible rotting animal carcasses – and even the bodies of dead enemy soldiers.

Blockade

A blockade stopped food getting in, or castle-dwellers getting out. It slowly starved the castle's inhabitants. In the meantime, attacking forces could stay in comfortable temporary timber or stone 'siege-castles', or in local church towers.

Halt! No one shall pass.

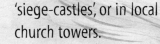

Undermining the castle walls

Tunnelling under the walls was effective and feared by defenders. A tunnel began out of bowshot, aiming to go under the castle wall or tower foundations. When brushwood fires were lit in the tunnel under the foundations, the walls often came tumbling down, as happened at Rochester, England in 1215.

A siege army needed many men – to cut down trees to make siege engines, to quarry stone for missiles, and to tunnel under the castle walls.

How did soldiers defend castles?

The defenders themselves had to think up tactics to outsmart their enemy. A concentric castle with a well and plenty of supplies could last for months, but they needed to break the siege.

What were the defenders' tactics?

There were a number of ways defenders could fight off a well-organised attack on their castle.

Corn grinding

▶ Long forked poles worked against direct assaults on the walls by pushing away ladders from castle walls.

▶ Crossbow bolts and longbow arrows were good weapons, because they could pass through attacking soldiers' armour.

Mats could put out fires in wooden castles, and deaden the power of battering rams.

▶ Murder holes (holes in the upper floor) in the gatehouse, allowed defenders to drop missiles or boiling liquid onto the enemy below.

Ammunition store

Well

How did they live under siege?

The people inside the besieged castle could grind their own corn, and always had a well full of water. They also had stored salted fish and meat, as well as beer and wine. If there was time before a siege, defenders brought cows, goats and sheep into the outer bailey.

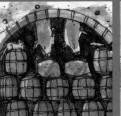

candles
firewood
charcoal
iron
rope
timber

Defenders sent out raids before sieges began, to try and capture the enemy's leader.

The castle needed plenty of food, water and ammunition.

Rationing helped the food last longer. Beer and wine was often safer to drink than well water, because boiled water had been used to make it.

Charge!

Defenders could creep out at night and set fire to the besiegers' supplies!

Run away! Retreat!

Someone has set fire to the food!

◀ Counter barrages (missiles) back to the enemy from soldiers in the castle worked quite well. In 1266 at Kenilworth, England, incoming and outgoing catapult missiles hit each other in mid-air!

A small number of men could get into the castle through its latrine chute. In 1204, some French soldiers entered Chateau Gaillard this way. Frightened defenders ran off and the whole army was let in.

▲ Counter-mining from inside the castle could intercept enemy miners, and stop them in their tracks. Wet moats also stopped attackers mining below the castle walls.

Where are the old castles?

By the 15th century, medieval times were drawing to a close. The old feudal loyalties were dying and in more peaceful times, fewer people wanted to live in castles. Many old castles were abandoned. Today most are in ruins, and visited only by tourists. Just a few are still used as homes.

▲ Many castles were not needed and fell into ruin.

What effect did guns have?

By the 16th century only the thickest walls – such as those of the huge gun forts built by England's King Henry VIII – could stand up to heavy cannon-fire. New weapons and artillery could completely destroy most castle walls.

◀ 17th century cannon fired iron cannon balls.

Why did people leave their castles?

Lords in late medieval times thought castles were too expensive, cold and uncomfortable to live in. England's rich, powerful lords wanted comfort as well as security. Their new castles looked traditional, but they built a comfortable courtyard house – a stately home – inside the concentric castle walls. Sometimes there were even fake machicolations.

▲ In the 15th century Raglan Castle in Wales looked like a palace. Now it is in ruin.

How did they make new castles comfortable?

During the late 16th century, builders added new, luxurious suites of rooms to the upper storeys of some castle's defensive gatehouses or in the wall towers. Beautiful gardens were created in the castle grounds, and some towers had large, cone-shaped roofs added later.

A selection of castle sites in Europe

Caerlaverock Castle, Scotland. This triangluar-shaped castle has two moats and was built c.1270.

Mespelbrunn Castle, Germany. Dating back to the 13th century, this castle was built in a valley and is surrounded by water.

The Tower of London, England. Built in 1100, the 'White Tower' had concentric walls and a moat added in the 13th century.

Karlstejn Castle, Czech Republic. This 14th century castle was re-built in the 19th century and is famous for its exterior.

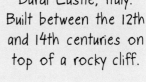

Harlech Castle, Wales. Built by Edward I, Harlech formed part of his iron ring of strategic castles.

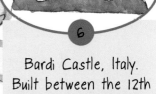

Bardi Castle, Italy. Built between the 12th and 14th centuries on top of a rocky cliff.

Castillo de los Cartagena, Spain. Built c.1400 by D Pedro de Cartagena.

Castle Ortenbourg, France. Built c.1260, the castle consists of a 5 storey keep and a high stone curtain wall.

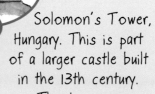

Solomon's Tower, Hungary. This is part of a larger castle built in the 13th century. The tower is hexagonal, and had a curtain wall added later.

Timeline

8th century Muslim 'Moors' invade Spain from North Africa, and begin building castles.

950 CE Normans begin building mainly timber castles in France.

998 CE Engineers fortify Antioch, near the Holy Land.

10th–11th century Saxon lords in England build fortified houses.

c.1050 The English king Edward the Confessor asks Normans to build a motte and bailey castle at Ludlow.

1066 William the Conqueror successfully invades England, winning the battle of Hastings. He builds castles in England, and parts of Wales and Scotland.

c.1070–1200 Castle builders in Britain and Europe put up great strong towers, which are later called 'keeps'.

1095 European Christians mount the first Crusade to the Holy Land. The Crusaders reach Constantinople, then capture Antioch and Jerusalem from the Muslim Saracens.

1142 Castle Kerak of Moab is built by the Crusaders to dominate the route taken by Muslims to attack Christian Crusaders in the Holy Land.

1142 Castle Krak des Chevaliers is surrendered to the Crusaders.

1147–1149 The 2nd failed Crusade.

1150–1250 Holy Roman Emperors build castles in Germany. Frederick of Hohestauffen builds castles in Italy.

1154–89 In England, Henry II builds and modernises castles.

1189–92 3rd Crusade.

1205 Krak des Chevaliers is rebuilt as the 'perfect' concentric castle.

1229 The 6th Crusade.

1248–54 The 7th Crusade (to Egypt).

1272-1307 England's feudal kingdom under Edward I spends huge sums of money building castles in north Wales.

13th century King Edward I and his army invade Scotland, and build castles.

1346 Cannon appear, so some castle builders add gunports to castle walls.

15th century The great age of castle building draws to a close. Many castles are abandoned by the 17th century.

Glossary

bailey

The outer courtyard protected by a strong wooden fence that surrounded early castles. An outer bailey, a term used later, referred to the narrow strip of land between the lower curtain wall and the higher inner wall of a concentric castle.

bribery

Offering someone money or a gift in return for something else. Bribery was sometimes used to break a siege; someone inside the castle was paid to leave a back door open.

concentric

The style of castle which featured an outer curtain wall and an inner wall, with a courtyard and other buildings in the centre. New concentric castles did not have a keep.

composite

Refering to something that is made up of different parts. A composite castle was a mixture of old and new structures that had been added or changed over the years.

feudal

A type of ruling system where people are governed and protected by a lord or king. In return, wealthier people who formed part of the lord's household might serve in his army. Poorer people worked on the lord's land and paid taxes.

fortified

When something is strengthened against an attack. The homes of wealthy families were fortified during the medieval period.

foundations

The prepared ground underneath a building. Castle foundations often consisted of levelled, compacted earth and stone.

garderobe

An old word for a private toilet or latrine.

Holy Land, the

Palestine; the area of land between the River Jordan and the Mediterranean Sea. It is called the Holy Land because that is where Christians believe many stories from the Bible occurred.

motte

The artificial mound of earth on which a timber tower stood. It was protected by a bailey.

siege

When an attacking army surrounds an enemy castle and blocks supplies to starve out the people inside. They also used siege machines to attack the castle, and other tactics. A siege could last a long time.

strategic

When something is planned, usually for a specific reason. Many castles were strategically placed. For example, many were built on high ground so they could control the surrounding land.

tactics

The diffferent ways soldiers are positioned to fight battles.

Index

barbican 18, 19, 20
building castles 8, 10–11, 16

cannon 23, 26, 28
castle types
  concentric 6, 7, 20–21, 22, 24, 26, 28, 29
  keep 7, 12, 13, 18, 20, 21, 27, 28
  motte and bailey 6, 12, 28, 29
  timber 6, 10, 23
Church, the 9
composite castle 18, 29
craftsmen 9, 10, 11
Crusades 6, 19, 21, 28
curtain wall 7, 13, 18, 19, 20, 21, 22

earth mounds 7, 12
Edward I 7, 11, 17, 21, 27, 28
England 6, 11, 17, 26, 27

feudal society 8, 26, 29
France 6, 7, 27

gatehouse 18, 19, 21, 24, 26

Holy Land, the 6, 19, 28, 29
household 14–15

Italy 6, 27, 28

kings and lords 6, 7, 8, 9, 10, 14, 16

machicolations 18, 19, 26
Master James of St George 21
medieval period or society 6, 8, 9, 26
Middle Ages 6
moat or ditch 7, 12, 15, 18, 19, 27

Moors 6, 7, 10, 17, 28
murder holes 24

Normans 6, 7, 12, 28
North Africa 6, 28

outer bailey 20

portcullis 18, 19

rooms 13, 14, 15
ruins 7, 26

siege 22, 23, 24, 25, 29
siege castles 23
siege machines 22, 23
Spain 6, 7, 10, 17, 27, 28
strategic planning 17, 29

tactics 22, 23, 24, 25, 29
taxes 8
towers 6, 7, 12, 18, 19, 20, 21, 26, 27, 28
towns 9

undermining 19, 23

Wales 6, 11, 17, 21, 27, 28
walls, also see curtain wall
  12, 13, 22, 24, 26
well 12, 13, 25
windows 12, 13
William the
  Conqueror 7, 22, 28